914.94
JNF

2/14

GEOGRAPHY OF THE WORLD

THE AWESOME

# ALPS

*By Barbara A. Somervill*

THE CHILD'S WORLD®
CHANHASSEN, MINNESOTA

Published in the United States of America by The Child's World®
PO Box 326, Chanhassen, MN 55317-0326
800-599-READ
www.childsworld.com

Content Adviser:
Mark Williams,
Associate Professor,
University of Colorado,
Boulder, Colorado

Photo Credits: Cover/frontispiece: Tim Thompson/Corbis
Interior: John Anderson/Animals Animals/Earth Scenes: 10, 18; Animals
Animals/Earth Scenes: 6 (Robert Comport), 12 (Barbara Von Hoffmann), 20
(Robert Maier), 21 (Peter Weimann); Corbis: 4 (Reuters), 7 (Sylvain Saustier), 8
(Marc Garanger), 13 (Premium Stock), 15 (Bettmann), 16 (Ric Ergenbright), 17
(ML Sinibaldi), 27 (Adam Woolfitt); Travelsite/Colasanti/Picture Desk: 22, 25.

The Child's World®: Mary Berendes, Publishing Director

Editorial Directions, Inc.: E. Russell Primm, Editorial Director; Melissa McDaniel,
Line Editor; Katie Marsico, Associate Editor; Judi Shiffer, Associate Editor and Library
Media Specialist; Matthew Messbarger, Editorial Assistant; Susan Hindman, Copy
Editor; Sarah E. De Capua and Lucia Raatma, Proofreaders; Marsha Bonnoit, Peter
Garnham, Terry Johnson, Olivia Nellums, Chris Simms, Katherine Trickle, and
Stephen Carl Wender, Fact Checkers; Tim Griffin/IndexServ, Indexer; Cian Loughlin
O'Day, Photo Researcher; Linda S. Koutris, Photo Selector; XNR Productions, Inc.,
Cartographer

The Design Lab: Kathleen Petelinsek, Design and Page Production

**Library of Congress Cataloging-in-Publication Data**
Somervill, Barbara A.
  The awesome Alps / by Barbara A. Somervill.
    p. cm. — (Geography of the world series)
  Includes index.
  ISBN 1-59296-330-7 (library bound : alk. paper) 1. Alps—Description and travel.
2. Alps—Civilization. 3. Mountain ecology—Alps. 4. Human ecology—Alps. 5.
Human geography—Alps. 6. Alps—Social life and customs. I. Title. II. Series.
  DQ823.5.S66 2004
  914.94'7—dc22                                          2004003723

# Table of Contents

# CHAPTER ONE

# THE ICE MAN

I n September 1991, Helmut and Erika Simon were hiking in the Alps along the border between Austria and Italy. Near the path, Erika spied a person lying in the ice. The person was dead. The Simons thought they had found a body from 10 or 20 years ago. They had no idea that their "ice man" would cause such a stir. No one imagined that the person had lived 5,300 years ago.

*Hikers in the Alps found this mummified body of a man who lived 5,300 years ago.*

Scientists quickly removed the body from the ice. The frozen man was remarkably well preserved. The scientists discovered that he had suffered a skull wound and three broken ribs. He had other injuries that appeared to be arrow wounds.

Fur, wood, and leather were lying near the frozen man's body. The man's hand held a crude ax. He carried a bow and 14 arrows. He also had **flints** for lighting fires.

The ice man's ancient clothes fell apart when they were exposed to the air. Enough bits remained, however, to show stitches along the seams. The man wore fur leggings, a fur cap, and grass-lined shoes. He had tattoos on his ankles and back.

Scientists thought that the ice man had frozen to death. But DNA tests done in 2003 showed that the ice man may have been murdered. They now believe he died from injuries related to being stabbed with a knife that was found with his body. Lying on the ground high in the Alps, his body became coated in ice and snow. And there he remained, for more than 5,000 years.

# CHAPTER TWO

# THE MAKING OF A MOUNTAIN RANGE

I t takes time for mountains to form. This process happens over millions and millions of years. The earth shaped mountains hundreds of millions of years ago. It builds new mountains even today.

Mountains are built in several different ways. Volcanoes, earthquakes, incredible pressure, and massive collisions build mountains.

*A massive collision built the Alps millions of years ago.*

*Long ago, these lush green hills were active, lava-spitting volcanoes.*

Most mountain ranges, including the Alps, result from a combination of these processes.

The Alps area has experienced three major mountain-building periods. The first happened 600 million years ago. Those mountains wore away long ago.

About 200 million years ago, a salt sea covered today's Alpine land. The seabed was slowly covered with animal skeletons, sand, and clay. Over hundreds of thousands of years, pressure on this material turned it into **sedimentary** rock. In time, the sea disappeared entirely. It had been replaced by mounds of sedimentary rock—the foundation of new mountains.

Then 65 million years ago, another set of mountains was created in a different way. It involved a change in the earth's crust. The continents and ocean floor make up the outer layer of earth, called the crust. The crust is not one unbroken layer like an orange peel. Instead, it has cracks and cuts. These cracks make the earth's crust more like a jigsaw puzzle. Each huge piece is called a

*Écrins National Park, France, features many stark, forbidding peaks.*

plate. Earth has about 20 different plates. Here's the important part: the plates move.

**WHAT IS A MASSIF?**
Several Alpine mountains are massifs. A massif is a main mountain in a range. In the Alps, these include Mont Blanc and the Matterhorn. A massif is actually a block of Earth's crust. The block has been pushed, twisted, and pressed to form particularly large peaks of a mountain range.

Try this: Spread a dish towel out on the kitchen counter. Place a saucer on each end of the dish towel. Slowly press on the saucers and push them toward each other. What happens? The dish towel puckers and folds. On a much larger scale, colliding plates create puckers and folds in the earth's crust. When the Eurasian Plate and the African Plate crashed together, they built the Alps.

This massive collision happened about 65 million years ago. For a mountain range, this is toddler age. The Appalachian Mountains in the eastern United States, in contrast, are between 290 million and 435 million years old.

Two basic features define a mountain range. The first is the environment it provides. The second is its **geology,** or makeup.

Mountains support a variety of plants and animals. The mix of living things changes depending on how high up the mountain they are. The foothills at the base of the Alps are covered with forests of pine, spruce, aspen, oak, maple, beech, and larch. These trees provide food and shelter for birds, insects, and mammals ranging from tiny shrews to large roe deer. Grassy foothills provide a different **habitat.** They support ground-nesting birds, insects, and rodents that live in underground burrows.

The timberline is the place on a mountain above which trees do not grow. **Tundra** lies above the timberline. Lichens, mosses, forbs, sedges, and grasses survive in the tundra. Mountain wildflowers, which are types of forbs, splash yellow and purple amid green grasses and ash-colored lichens. Birds and rodents thrive in the tundra, but few large animals live there.

*Wildflowers sprinkle color through this Alpine meadow.*

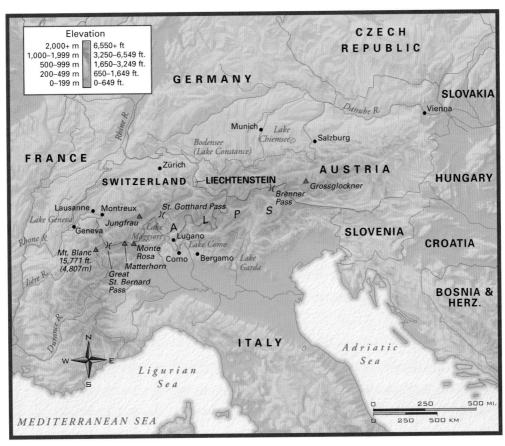

*A map of the Alps*

Even farther up the mountains, **glaciers** cover some of the ground. The weather there is so cold that the snow and ice never melts. About 1,300 glaciers blanket today's Alps.

Scientists tell how a mountain formed from its geology. Volcanic mountains have rocks made from cooled **magma,** such as granite or quartz. Other mountains have sedimentary rock, such as sandstone

*This quarry yields marble for building stone, tombstones, and sculptures.*

SO SAYS LEONARDO
In the 15th century, the artist and scientist Leonardo da Vinci described climbing a peak in the Alps. He wrote, "The sun as it fell on the mountain was far brighter here than in the plains below."

or limestone. This kind of mountain has rock in layers, like a cake. Pressure and heat can also change one type of rock into another. For example, limestone under intense pressure and heat forms marble. Such rocks are called **metamorphic.**

The Alps feature all three types of rock. Many Alps are made mainly of limestone. Others have granite. Still others are made of metamorphic rocks called gneiss (NICE) and schist.

# CHAPTER THREE

# ABOUT THE ALPS

The Alps dominate south-central Europe. They include all or part of seven countries: Austria, France, Germany, Italy, Liechtenstein, Slovenia, and Switzerland. For people who live in the Alps, snow, ice, and long winters are a normal part of life.

*Berchtesgaden, Germany, is postcard-pretty after a winter snowfall.*

The Alps form a barrier between Italy to the south and Switzerland and Austria to the north. This region is called the Central Alps and features the tallest peaks in the range. France is home to Mont Blanc, the highest peak in the Alps. It rises 15,771 feet (4,807 meters) above sea level. Monte Rosa, the Matterhorn, and Jungfrau are high peaks that rise in Switzerland. Another tall Alpine peak is Grossglockner, which looms over Austria's Tirol region.

Some of Europe's most beautiful rivers and lakes lie in the Alps. The Rhine flows 700 miles (1,100 kilometers) through Germany and the Netherlands and then empties into the North Sea. The Isére and Durance rivers twist and turn through Alpine valleys before joining the Rhone in southern France. The Danube, Europe's second-longest river, crosses Austria on its way to the Black Sea.

The Alps host more than a thousand lakes. The scenic beauty of these lakes has

## GREAT SAINT BERNARD PASS

The Great Saint Bernard Pass cuts through the Alps on the border between Italy and Switzerland. During the 12th and 13th centuries, a group of monks lived beside the pass. The monks often searched for travelers lost in brutal snowstorms. They took their huge dogs with them to help search. The dogs became known as Saint Bernards.

*A lone swan glides across the waters of Lake Geneva, Switzerland.*

inspired poets, novelists, and artists. Switzerland's Lake Geneva straddles the border between France and Switzerland. Both Geneva and Lausanne, Switzerland, sprawl beside the lakeshore.

Northern Italy's Lake District boasts Lake Maggiore, Lake Como, and Lake Garda. The nearby Italian cities of Bergamo, Como, and Lugano prosper from tourism in the region.

Southern Germany is the site of the Bodensee and Chiemsee, two bustling vacation spots. The lakes are an easy drive from Munich, Germany, and Zürich, Switzerland.

# CHAPTER FOUR

# PLANTS AND ANIMALS OF THE ALPS

Unlike other major mountain ranges such as the Andes or Himalayas, the Alps have been heavily developed for tens of thousands of years. Long ago, people cleared away Alpine forests to make way for farms. Meadows became wheat fields or cow pastures. Recently, forests

*A farmer harvests hay in the shadows of Alpine peaks.*

*Alpine meadows provide comfortable homes for hares, marmots, and field mice.*

have fallen to bulldozers as people develop new ski runs and resorts. In the Alps, little room is left for native wildlife or plants.

The remaining Alpine meadows come alive each spring with white edelweiss, blue columbine, and clusters of yellow laburnum. Orange lilies line mountain streams beside purple belladonna and deep blue trumpet gentians. Delicate alpenroses and rugged Alpine sea holly are named after their mountain home. But surprisingly, few of these wildflowers are native to the Alps.

*Pine and spruce grow up to the timberline on the slopes of Mont Blanc, Switzerland.*

Pine, spruce, and fir grow as high up as 9,200 feet (2,800 m). In the French and Italian Alps near the Mediterranean Sea, olive trees, cypress, and larches spread their leaves to the warming sun. Northern forests host gray-trunked beeches and spindly oaks.

The Alpine timberline lies at roughly 9,000 feet (2,700 m) above sea level. Above this line, glacier crowfoot and the strangely named sneezewort grow on the Alpine tundra. These plants, along with lichens, mosses, and sedges, can be found up to about 14,000 feet (4,300 m). Tundra plant life lies close to the ground. This helps protect it from wind, frost, and loss of water.

Animals move up and down the mountains according to the

season. In the summer, high meadows host a range of birds, insects, rodents, and butterflies. Large plant-eating animals such as ibex, chamois, and mouflon graze on wildflowers and tall grasses.

As winter grips the mountains, many animals move down into the protection of the subalpine forests. There, they can find food. The dense forest shields animals from the wind and snow.

Some animals live all year in the tundra. Marmots, snow voles, and mountain hares survive in underground burrows. Marmots sleep away the long winter months. Mountain hares grow a thick fur coat for protection from the cold.

Few large **predators** live in the Alps. Long ago, people in the Alps killed off wolves and lynxes to protect their herds of cattle and goats. Smaller predators, such as weasels and stoats, thrive in Alpine forests. They feed on hares, shrews, and mice.

*Scampering field mice better watch out when this young goshawk is on the hunt for dinner.*

Most Alpine birds do not move to warmer regions during the winter. Birds such as golden eagles, goshawks, and eagle owls find plenty of prey to feed themselves and their chicks throughout the cold months. Jackdaws call out a harsh "chak, chak" as they feed on berries or insects. Marmots and shrews hide from red kites circling above Alpine meadows. Black woodpeckers rat-a-tat-tat to shake insects from their hiding places in pine and spruce bark.

Today, goshawks, ibex, mouflon, and other creatures depend on national preserves to safeguard their habitats. Curved-horn ibex climb the steep cliffs of the Swiss National Park in Graubünden. Vultures,

*Berchtesgaden National Park preserves wildlife in the northern Alps.*

golden eagles, chamois, and marmots have all been reintroduced to the

park wilderness.

Other nature preserves and parks can be found in Italy, France,

Germany, and Slovenia. Italy's Val Grande Park is a wilderness region

where animals and plants live in their natural state. Visitors view roe

deer, chamois, golden eagles, and vipers, which are a type of snake.

Germany's Berchtesgaden is the oldest protected preserve in Europe.

The park features stunning wildflowers, blue hares, and black grouse.

# CHAPTER FIVE

# PEOPLE OF THE ALPS

P eople have lived in the Alps for thousands of years. Early settlements along the Danube date from 100,000 to 150,000 years ago. By 10,000 B.C., groups of humans lived in many Alpine valleys and meadows.

Although the Alps are difficult to travel over, that did not always stop invading armies. Just more than 2,000 years ago, Roman armies crossed the Alps. By 15 B.C., Roman control extended as far north as the Danube. Many other people also traveled in the Alps, establishing villages, towns, and cities throughout the range.

Today, the lives of people in the Alps are the same as those of other Europeans. Modern transportation

*Chamonix, France, is a popular*
*ski resort near Mont Blanc.*

connects Alpine cities and villages to the rest of Europe. Air, train, and road travel make transportation to and from the Alps easy. The passes used in ancient times—Brenner, Saint Bernard, and Saint Gotthard— are main routes through the Alps. Heavy snows may interrupt travel. But the snow is removed quickly, and few roads remain closed for long.

Most people in the Alps have both home telephones and cell phones. Personal computers are popular, and many people are connected to the Internet. Most homes have radios and televisions. Austria has more than 60 radio stations and 51 television stations. Switzerland has more than 115 radio stations and 110 television stations. Shows are broadcast in German, French, Italian, and Romansh, a Swiss dialect.

People of many different backgrounds live in the Alps. Most people are of German heritage. But French, Italians, Slovenes, Turks, Croatians, Czechs, and Slovaks also live there. Switzerland has three official languages—German, French, and Italian—because the people living there have such varied ethnic backgrounds.

People who live in the Alps have the same jobs as other Europeans.

They're employed as doctors, lawyers, bankers, factory workers, and farmers. Alpine cities such as Geneva, Switzerland; Vienna, Austria; and Munich, Germany, are major banking and industrial centers. Machinery, watches, and medical equipment are all produced in the Alps. Ceramics and processed foods are also major Alpine moneymakers.

Farming still plays a big role in the Alps. Livestock provide quality beef, lamb, cheeses, milk, and butter. Most farms are confined to a small meadow or valley. Crops grown in the Alps include wheat, barley, potatoes, grapes, and olives.

Five Alpine nations—Germany, France, Austria, Italy, and Slovenia—belong to the **European Union.** The European Union promotes Europe's economy and works to create a closer relationship among the member nations. Switzerland and Liechtenstein have not joined the European Union, but they still trade with other European countries.

**LIECHTENSTEIN**

**Liechtenstein is the smallest European nation. It is about the size of Washington, D.C. The country depends heavily on its friendship with Switzerland. Instead of printing its own money and postage stamps, Liechtenstein uses Swiss money and stamps.**

# CHAPTER SIX

# THE CULTURE OF THE ALPS

Traditions and festivals in the Alps differ from location to location. People with different ethnic backgrounds have different customs.

One common link across the Alps is religion. Many Alpine families are Roman Catholic. People celebrate

**SUNDIALS**
In the southern Alps, many buildings have decorative sundials. These decorations include pictures of birds, flowers, the sun, or the moon. Often, advice related to time is carved into the sundials. One might say, "Passersby, remember as you go past that everything passes as I pass."

*This tiny church in Switzerland offers a quiet retreat for Alpine travelers.*

religious events such as Christmas, Easter, and saints' days as a community. In Slovenia, national holidays include Whitsunday, Assumption Day, and the Feast of All Souls. In Germany, New Year's Eve is called the Feast of Saint Silvester.

Not all feasts and festivals have religious connections. Many Alpine towns also celebrate music and art. Salzburg, Austria, is famed for its classical music festivals. Italians love opera, and jazz jam fests bring a buzz to Montreux, Switzerland. Christmas fairs and open markets give craftspeople a chance to sell their wares. Blown glass, painted ceramic figures, carved wooden statues, and fine leather goods are for sale at German arts festivals. Carved wooden tables, chairs, chests, and jewelry cases draw the eye of shoppers in the French Alps.

Food plays a central role in almost every Alpine celebration. In Italy, it's dumplings, sausages, risotto, and veal. In Austria, diners choose goulash or a veal dish called Wiener schnitzel. Germans also enjoy their sausages, smoked ham, cheese, and apples. A German buffet might include *brotzeitteller,* a platter filled with smoked meats, cheeses, and pickles. Switzerland enjoys the treats of all of its neighbors. Sausages, roasts, fried potatoes, cheeses, and some of the world's best chocolate grace Swiss dinner tables.

The people of the Alps celebrate all the common events of life. A wedding or the birth of a child brings family and friends together. In

*This bakery in Kitzbuhel, Austria, produces delicious breads, pastries, and cakes.*

years past in the French Alps, if someone died during the winter, the body was covered with snow and stored on the roof! The body was buried after the spring thaw. Family and friends gathered to share the experience. Like people everywhere, those in the Alps honor both life and death.

# Glossary

**European Union (yu-ruh-PEE-uhn YOON-yuhn)** The European Union is a group of European nations that work together to help their economies and maintain peace. Many members of the European Union now use the same money.

**flints (FLINTZ)** Flints are rock tools used to make a spark to start a fire. The frozen body discovered in the Alpine ice was carrying flints.

**geology (jee-OL-uh-jee)** Geology is a science that deals with the history of of the earth and what rocks can reveal about that. Scientists can learn how a mountain formed from its geology.

**glaciers (GLAY-shurz)** Glaciers are huge sheets of moving ice. There are more than 1,000 glaciers atop the Alps.

**habitat (HAB-uh-tat)** A habitat is a place where a plant or animal normally lives. The grassy foothills of the Alps provide habitat for ground-nesting birds.

**magma (MAG-muh)** Magma is the melted rock inside the earth. When magma cools, it becomes igneous rock.

**metamorphic (met-uh-MOR-fik)** A metamorphic rock is a type of rock formed by high heat and pressure. Gneiss and schist are two types of metamorphic rock.

**predators (PRED-uh-turz)** Predators are animals that hunt and eat other animals. Weasels and stoats are predators that live in the Alps.

**sedimentary (sed-uh-MEN-tuh-ree)** Sedimentary rock is rock formed from the remains of eroded mountains, including sand, clay, rock, salts, and animal remains. Limestone is a type of sedimentary rock.

**sundials (SUHN-dye-uhlz)** Sundials are tools that show the time of day by the shadow cast by a pin. Many buildings in the southern Alps have sundials.

**tundra (TUHN-druh)** Tundra is a treeless region in the far north or on the upper portion of a mountain. Mosses and lichens live in the Alpine tundra.

# An Alps Almanac

**Extent**
    Length: About 750 miles (1,200 km)
    Width: About 160 miles (260 km)

**Continent:** Europe

**Countries:** Austria, France, Germany, Italy, Liechtenstein, Slovenia, and Switzerland

**Major ranges:** Central Alps, Eastern Alps, and Western Alps

**Major rivers:** Aare, Danube, Durance, Hinterrhein, Isère, Oglio, Rhine, and Rhone

**Major lakes:** Bodensee, Chiemsee, Como, Geneva, Maggiore, and Zurich

**Major cities:** Innsbruck, Salzburg, Vienna (Austria); Annecy, Chambery, Grenoble (France); Garmisch Partenkirchen, Munich, Rosenheim (Germany); Bergamo, Brescia, Como (Italy); Ljubljana (Slovenia); Basel, Geneva, Zurich (Switzerland)

**Major languages:** French, German, Italian, and Slovenian

**High peaks:**

| | | |
|---|---|---|
| Mont Blanc | 15,771 feet | (4,807 m) |
| Monte Rosa | 15,203 feet | (4,634 m) |
| Matterhorn | 14,692 feet | (4,478 m) |
| Jungfrau | 13,642 feet | (4,158 m) |
| Grossglockner | 12,457 feet | (3,797 m) |

**Parks and preserves:** Hohe Tuaern, Hohe Wand, Karwendel (Austria); Ècrins, Mercantour, Vanoise (France); Berchtesgaden (Germany); Abruzzo, Gran Paradiso, Stelvio, Val Grande (Italy); Triglav (Slovenia); Swiss National Park (Switzerland)

**Natural resources:** Bauxite, hydroelectric power, iron ore, lignite coal, timber, and salt

**Native birds:** Black grouse, golden eagles, goshawks, jackdaws, kites, owls, vultures, and woodpeckers

**Native mammals:** Blue hares, chamois, deer, ibex, marmots, mouflons, shrews, stoats, voles, and weasels

**Native reptiles:** Vipers

**Native plants:** Alpenroses, Alpine sea hollies, beeches, belladonna, columbines, cypresses, edelweiss, firs, larches, lichens, lilies, mosses, oaks, olives, pines, sedges, spruces, and trumpet gentian

# The Alps in the News

| | |
|---|---|
| **600 million years ago** | The first mountain-building period in Alpine region takes place. |
| **200 million years ago** | The Alpine region is covered by a salt sea. |
| **65 million years ago** | A collision between the Eurasian Plate and African Plate builds modern Alps. |
| **100,000– 150,000 years ago** | Groups of humans live along the Danube. |
| **10,000 B.C.** | People move into Alpine valleys and foothills. |
| **15 B.C.** | The Roman Empire extends all the way over the Alps to the Danube. |
| **A.D. 1100–1300** | Monks who live near the Great Saint Bernard Pass search for lost travelers. |
| **1719** | Liechtenstein declares its independence. |
| **1867** | Railroad tracks are completed through Brenner Pass, connecting Austria and Italy. |
| **1871** | A railroad tunnel is completed at Mount Cenis. |
| **1914** | Switzerland founds the Swiss National Park, one of the first in Europe; Switzerland organizes the Red Cross to help soldiers during World War I (1914–1918). |
| **1935** | Italy establishes Stelvio National Park to preserve wildlife. |
| **1939–1945** | World War II (1939–1945) engulfs all of Europe. |
| **1950** | The French propose a plan for the European Union. |
| **1967** | Switzerland holds the first Montreux Jazz Festival. |
| **1978** | Germany founds a national park at Berchtesgaden. |
| **1979** | France establishes a national park at Mount Mercantour. |
| **1991** | A 5,300-year-old ice man is found in Austrian Alps; Slovenia declares independence from Yugoslavia. |
| **2002** | Switzerland becomes a member of the United Nations. |

# How to Learn More about the Alps

## At The Library

### NONFICTION

Ake, Anne. *Austria*. San Diego: Lucent Books, 2001.

Hammond, Paula. *Italy and Switzerland*. Broomall, Pa.: Mason Crest Publishers, 2002.

Harris, Pamela K. *Switzerland*. Chanhassen, Minn.: The Child's World, 2001.

Stein, R. Conrad. *Austria*. Danbury, Conn.: Children's Press, 2000.

### FICTION

Dahlberg, Maurine F. *Playing to the Angel*. New York: Puffin Books, 2002.

Spyri, Johanna. *Heidi*. New York: Aladdin Library, 2000.

## On the Web

VISIT OUR HOME PAGE FOR LOTS OF LINKS ABOUT THE ALPS:

*http://www.childsworld.com/links.html*

Note to Parents, Teachers, and Librarians: We routinely verify our Web links to make sure they're safe, active sites—so encourage your readers to check them out!

## Places to Visit or Contact

AUSTRIAN NATIONAL TOURIST OFFICE

11601 Wilshire Boulevard

Los Angeles, CA 90025

FRENCH GOVERNMENT

TOURIST BUREAU

610 Fifth Avenue

New York, NY 10020

GERMAN NATIONAL TOURIST OFFICE

122 East 42nd Street

New York, NY 10068

ITALIAN TOURIST OFFICE

630 Fifth Avenue

New York, NY 10020

# Index

## About the Author

**Barbara A. Somervill** is the author of many books for children. She loves learning and sees every writing project as a chance to learn new information or gain a new understanding. Somervill grew up in New York State, but she has also lived in Toronto, Canada; Canberra, Australia; California; and South Carolina. She currently lives with her husband in Simpsonville, South Carolina.